Cheraw Chronicles

Cheraw Chronicles

Frank Motley

Cheraw Chronicles
Copyright @2018 by Frank Motley

All rights reserved. No part of this book may be reproduced or transmitted in any form or by any means without written permission from the author.

If you purchased this book without a cover you should be aware that this book is stolen property. It was reported as "unsold and destroyed" to the publisher and neither the author nor the publisher has received payment for the "stripped book."

Photos
Front cover photograph of African masks taken in Dakar Senegal. Back cover photograph is *The Door of No Return* taken on Goree Island, Senegal. Both photos were taken by the author.

ISBN: 978-1-7325724-0-9

Printed in USA

Alpha Lion Press
Bloomington, Indiana
2018

Preface

Unashamedly, I confess to a love of poetry. I confess to quietly and consistently writing it in my spare time. Throughout college, law school, marriage, five kids and nineteen grandkids, I have blocked out minutes here and there to write poetry.

I was not ashamed of my passion but I was self conscious about describing myself as a poet. The word sounded so pretentious. As if I had some special insight or knowledge of the world. I do not.

What I had – hopefully still do – is a uniquely personal way of experiencing the world. I felt more like a journalist – someone who was more observing than pontificating.

Whether I have been successful in communicating my view of the world is something that you will have to decide.

I hope one or two of the poems in this book bring a smile to your face or even raise an eyebrow. I would not mind your hating one or two, either. The worse thing would be that you were indifferent or unmoved by any of them.

Whether these are good or bad poems will not be determined by some literary critic in some arcane journal but by you, the reader. You know what you like and what you don't. You know what moves you.

The overarching theme of the poems in this book is family. For me, appreciating family began in Cheraw, South Carolina. The local newspaper was called *The Cheraw Chronicle* so I have borrowed that title as a reminder of those beginnings.

The gestation of these poems has been long. I began some of them in 1967. They are like my children. They have been spoiled and sheltered. And like grown children who have stayed too long in their parents' attic, it is time for them to "leave home." Time for them to grow up.

So with this publication, I have put them out. Ready or not, the poems must make a way on their own. I hope I have prepared them well and that the world and you the reader do not treat them too badly.

Frank Motley
September 2018

Dedication

To all my family, but especially to Uncle Wilbert and Aunt Gloria.

Thank you to all my friends who emerged from my experiences at

Minisink Order of the Feather
The New Hampton School
Columbia University
Amherst College
Indiana University
Alpha Phi Alpha Fraternity

To Mike Lacopo who mentored me at a critical juncture in my life. To Tom Diehl who mentored my brother at a critical time in his. To Jennifer Bohrnstedt who, by word and example, encouraged me. To Lawrence Aaron whose constructive criticism challenged me and made the poems (if not me) better.

And to my Homeboys (you know who you are…)

Contents

Sarah	1
John At Church	2
Grandma	3
Mister Frank	4
Lack History	7
Past My Heart	9
Whist With My Sis	11
Pee Dee Church Anniversary	14
Strange Root	16
Wearing His Scar	17
Black Attack	18
Black History	19
The Confederacy	20
Discovery	21
Galaxy Gazing	22
God's In Trouble	24
Ho	26
Icebergs at the Equator	27
To Inez	28
Life on the Curb	38
Made Men	39
Making America Great Again	40
For Milton	42
Baller	44
Original G	45
Watermelon	46
Spanish Driving Lessons	47
Denise	48
Homecoming	50

It is the Principle	51
To Sigmund	53
Who is Cousin Henry?	54
An Evening Among Georgia Fir	55
Dinner At Alecia's	57
Jim's Alexis & Me	58
Tissues	60
Lucky	61
Grits and Syrup	63
Happy Young	65
TLC	66
All Orphans Are Brothers	67
She, Like Her Blue Jeans	68
Pictures, the Clothes	69
Evil Evened	70
The Beatitudes	71

Sarah

Scrubbed floors
Cleaned toilets
Ironed clothes
Jobs of little joy
To earn college money
For John L, Sweet,
June & her precious Baby Boy.

A pillar in the church,
The rock in our lives.
Hard facade
Heart of marmalade.

Country smart,
Not been to school.
Had to work to eat,
Care for others,
Put shoes on tiny feet

A life lived in the shadow of
Cotton fields and the old sawmill.

A believer
In God and herself.
Grandmother was sure
One of them would get the job done.

A belief that strong
Had to be passed along.

Worked hard.
Loved hard.
More Old Testament than New.
What we learned has remained True.
You take care of God and He will take care of you.

John at church

A single touch
Filled the cathedral
Heavenly notes
Sped tears
Rolling cheek ward
To tongue
Salt taste
Solution
Ageless

What his mamma taught
He had not forgot

Grandma

My grandma
Used to always
Remind me:

"Boy, the Lord's eye is on the sparrow..."

And I used to believe her
(Grandma never lied to me)

The Lord's eye *is* on the sparrow, I thought.
(And prayed) And thought some more.

It wasn't 'till I was older
When I came north
That I discovered:

I ain't no sparrow...

And his eye on me,
Didn't stop no hunter.

Grandma never lied to me,
But then, grandma never had been
this far up north either.

Mister Frank

Mister Frank,
My father's father,
His brother's too.
My grandma's husband
My cousin's uncle
And my grandfather, too.

I knew church was important
Because granddaddy dressed up to go there
Grandma went to Pee Dee
So where grandpa went must have been extra special.

Grandpa wore overalls everyday
Except Sunday.
He rarely wore shoes,
His feet were callus enough –
His hands, too,
Sandpaper
Vice-grip.

Doing and reading
Never talking.
He did not share much
He spoke in the daily sacrifice
Of working in the mill
And planting in the fields

He named his mule after his wife.
(Not sure who should feel complimented)

Sang in the choir,
Read the newspaper daily,
A whiz in math.

Fried baloney for breakfast
Sawyer,
Carpenter,
Farmer,

At core
He did not need more
Family, church, and a good mule.

The following may help in reading the poem.

South Carolina, part of the original Province of Carolina, was founded in 1663 when King Charles II gave the land to eight noble men known as The Lords Proprietors.

Settled by the English in 1670, South Carolina became the eighth state to ratify the U.S. constitution in 1788. Its early economy was largely agricultural, benefitting from the area's fertile soil. Plantation farmers relied on the slave trade for cheap labor to maximize their profits. By 1730, people of African descent made up two thirds of the colony's population. South Carolina became the first state to secede from the union in 1861, and was the site of the first shots of the Civil War–the shelling of the federally held Fort Sumter by Confederate troops on April 12, 1861.

Famous South Carolinians include musicians James Brown, Chubby Checker and Dizzy Gillespie, novelist Pat Conroy, boxer Joe Frazier, tennis champion Althea Gibson, politician Jesse Jackson and long-serving U.S. Senator Strom Thurmond.

Date of Statehood: *May 23, 1788*
Capital: *Columbia*
Population: *4,625,364 (2010)*
Size: *32,021 square miles*
Nickname(s): *Palmetto State*
Motto: *Dum Spiro Spero (While I Breathe, I Hope)*
Tree: *Palmetto*
Flower: *Yellow Jessamine*
Bird: *Carolina Wren*

Lack History

Something is missing.
White not the only color
In God's vision.
The monochrome world
They suggest is surely not best.
What about us – the myriad rest?
No need to fuss.
God will take care of us.
Still, little time to waste.
The pimento of Truth
Will improve the taste.

There are hints all around.
Whistling through the trees,
A drum beat on the ground.

After the West was tamed,
Where are the Indians for whom
Cheraw was named?

Slavery

Dum Spiro Spero *was probably first muttered*
In the bowels of a slave ship long ago shuttered.

"While I breathe I hope,"
Despite slavers' tight rope.

Civil War

Eighth to ratify but the first to secede.
Was human bondage so organic a need?

Traitors then, traitors now.
Say it loud!
Ft. Sumter is nothing
Of which to be proud.

The decrescent moon and the palmetto tree
Of the Secessionist Flag do not represent me!

Then

What tragic tales could the mighty Pee Dee pour forth?
Stories of slaves, their families sneaking their journey north.

Long before the magnificent Cheraw State Park,
Many had to leave (or grieve) to make their mark

How long was Long High? And where has Coulter gone?
Who are Cheraw's white heroes and what good have they done?

Who does it honor for white boys – now Black ones - to call themselves 'Braves?"
If the real ones were hunted, killed - fancy condominiums built on their graves?

Kumbaya moments are rare and short lived.
Carolina has too little love to share or to give.

Now

Eighth to ratify but first to secede.
How much more white history does one have to read?

Past My Heart

I knew I was loved
Because I knew the location -

Past My Heart

A few feet from the rainbow

Heaven

The place my grandmother used to always pray about

Her heart - as big as we needed -

We were eight, seven, and six
When momma died.

One day, the sun just
Dropped.

Grandma picked it up
And saved it for us.

She taught us
Love without touch.
Sacrifice in silence.
Only a foot rub in the evening
as salve for not being retired,
Not resting in old age,
Back on duty,
Teaching we the unlearned.

Delayed props.
Muffled appreciation.

One day on the bench,
It came to him:
Why he swept the yard.

Ain't no love
Like love
Past your heart.

Whist With My Sis

You may kidnap me anytime.
Take me into a room where Cards are sublime.

Where No's take out specials
And one always leads with trump
Where joy is perpetual
And a good kitty is all you need to get over the hump

Ironic trump supporters devoted to getting the kitty.
For some men – this represents one's whole life's work!
Ain't that a pity?

For others, stopping Boston is well worth the pass.
They hate the weather and are glad the Celtics came in last.

The cards sweat and are hard to deal.
Like merchants at a flea market,
The card players swarm, looking to steal.

The cards are like drunken Greek gods run amuck
They do not pardon, parole, or take kindly to Luck.

More praying at a whist game than in church.
More promises of the good life than supervisors at work.

Bidding on a hunch and a prayer
That their partner has what's missing from the Kitty's lair

Saving the ace in hopes it falls in place.

What led? What was the bid she said?

All I need is one book to stop
The ravaging of the good and leaving Evil on top.

The Good Book indeed –
Just one book – is all I need.
Heaven sent, God lent.

A moment of extreme joy
Should she gorilla or act coy?

Check bid - don't want to renege.

Five or four?
I wish I had more.
A bid I can't make
Unless the Kitty has cake.

Do I feel lucky, Clint?
Or has my luck been spent?
Whose turn to learn
Bid wrong, get burned?

Holding those cards and getting the kitty,
Feeling sorry for the opponents cause
What's about to happen ain't gonna be pretty.

No pity, Vickie's got the kitty.
As if a sign from God.
The Kitty has all she needs to gut the hog.
From Durham to Cape Cod.
Near enough to Boston,
To see the smog
With a wink to her partner,
She begins the slaughter.

Not talking across the table,
That would be odd.
"But warm hearts and shiny rings are ever true.
Hooved Feet and black shovels are interesting and new"

"My cardiologist, on the way to his country club,
Dug on my ring. I thanked him and gave him a hug."

Smiles all round as last card falls down.
Made or not, the game has got to stop.
The points close.

The winners will boast
'bout their prowess at cards
When we all know
It is not them:
But the Will of the Gods.

Pee Dee Church Anniversary

More than a river.
Lifetimes and generations
Of family love
For the Giver of All.
Good and bad
Pass under His gaze.
We being amazed.
Indeed,
We being
Is amazing.

Pee Dee is more than the rock
On which God built a church.

It is the Godness
That flows through our veins.
An inheritance that generations will reap, unaware,
The hours of prayer,
The nourished soil on which
The cotton grew.
And the mill work
Ennobling the many and the few.

Sunday – the day of rest and reflection –
On Pharaoh's Plantation,
Earthly slaved
But Pee Dee saved.

His mercy abounds
Hiding us from the hounds.

Deep is the river.
Deeper still our love.
Learned in the pews
And parish of reverends
    - Old and new.

We stand in awe

Pee Dee of Cheraw

Sarah believed.
We believed because
She believed.
Enough
For our whole tribe.

One hundred and fifty years of watching God
Teaching fools
Mammon on earth
Unequal to
Inheritance at birth.

Right from wrong
Taught in gospel and song.

So many good men and women
Have worshiped and prayed in these pews.
How can one not see and hear - be glad and rejoice -
At (ah, yes) the Good News!

Strange Root

My people have
    axed
        more questions
            than your people
                have hung
                    dangling
                        participles...

Wearing his scar

*She was not always Victoria
Ella's little girl, Vicki, once
Played with matches
Out of sight but under
Her brother's assigned vigilance.*

*The sundress aflame,
Her cry out in pain,
His sister on fire.*

*The flames he smothered
Seared their souls together
- forever.*

*He would never forget,
Having forgot.*

Black Attack

I went to my black barber
    and he told me about his Jewish
        lawyer
I went to my black grocer
    and he told me about this
        Italian bakery
I went to my black cook
    and he told me about this great
        Chinese restaurant
I went to my black minister
    and he told me all about a
        White Jesus...

That's when I stopped going to Church
    and moved cross town,
    so as not to be confused
    by black people...

Black History

It is not for the want of trying
That we have been left out.
(Is it because many want to forget
The evil that they were all about?)

We have always been here –
In the kitchen, in the yard,
On the farm, working hard,
In the mines, and on the range,
In the stockyard and the cotton exchange.

Harvesting, cooking, and serving the food.
Trying to be accepted, hoping for the good.
Is it too much to ask for a seat at the table?
After three hundred years, have we not proved able?

Who picked the cotton on which they got so rich?
Who tilled the field and built the house brick by brick?
Who tended to their children and nursed them when they were sick?
Who fought wars, went home, and on whose uniform they spit?

The sweat equity of our forebears made America.
But this they would like to forget.
If remembered, they would have to pay the overdue debt.

We've never been paid near half what we are worth.
We probably won't collect our reward here on earth.
We won't get that which we were entitled from birth.

But at least stop lying about us being lazy.
Stop lying, cursing us and driving us crazy.

Historians are supposed to be truthful.
Equality is as necessary as it is beautiful.

The Confederacy

Why perpetuate the lie?
Face the truth, let the lie die:
The South was wrong to fight to keep slaves.
Nothing noble about it.
Confederate generals were traitors and knaves.

The stars and bars need to come down.
Discarded. Cast out and the ignominiously drowned.
The South should have lost – on more than paper.
Good must triumph over evil.
And not hide or turn to vapor

As one travels throughout the Southland,
You see so many generals on horses that it is so hard to understand.
To the children of slaves it is a horrendous eye sore.
So many generals, you wonder who won the war.

The world has been made great by Black men and White.
For every Caesar on the left, there is a Hannibal on the right.

Discovery

I turned sixty the other day,
And there was no parade,
No headline banner,
No shout-out on BET
But it was ok.
I learned something nifty
On the way to turning sixty:
I don't want you to freak out
Or think I am being crabby
But Truth is
I don't need
Anyone's permission
To be happy.

Galaxy Gazing

God explain,
So I can understand,
What Job did wrong?

God explain,
So I can understand,
That Billy Holiday song.

Strange fruit
Yields unruly cells

i.

There but for Fortune go I
(& When Fortune ducked around the corner)
There go me!

*Why **can't** I ask for whom the bell tolls?*

ii.

Two people face each other
One has no shoes, the other no feet.
You are one of the two.
Dare you look down?

iii.

Which is trump?

I don't want to die
                    Or

I want to live?

iv.

At some point Beyoncé wins
And you join the audience
And applaud quietly,
Remembering
That feeling she rents.

v.

We wear the mask....
Buy new hair...nails...
Change eye color...
Get nose & boob jobs...
Are any of us really real?

Our reality is not the flesh -
But the unfaded memories
Of deep laughter and recognition,
The comfort of true friendship

We are
The love in others' hearts
And the smile on their faces

vi.

After you have gone through the stages
And arrived at Acceptance,
There will come a peace
And love...
That only you, Job, and
What's-his-name can understand.

As for me, I am just trying to hang around
No cross, no crown.

God's in trouble

Every night he drives home to a lonely house,
Absent the melody and the warming smile of his bride turned spouse.
"Hollis! Oh Hollis!" she would call and he knew he was home
Forgotten trash, dirty dishes, abandoned clothes, or perhaps the forgotten oil puddle...
Hollis-Oh-Hollis would only appear to be in trouble.

But tonight, and last night,
And the night before
He walked through the door
Meeting only the quiet he abhorred.

Too much hospital air
& too little sleep
& too much distressing
& too many promises to keep

The hum of the machines
And the breathing gasps
Of the woman
He loves,
Shot up
Cut up
Hurt up

The weight of waiting,
Witnessing ...

There are not enough drugs
To dull this pain.
Not enough plastic
To hide these scars.

Hollis is not Job.
God is in trouble tonight.

If Christ had the nerve
He would enter the ring

Take off his long white robe and
In this cool night air,
Hollis would teach him a thing or two
About fighting fair…

Ho

Ho Chi Min died today
While the Cisco Kid lives on.
Girl of the big breast and stingy kiss,
Tell me, tell me please,
What do I do with my love for you?

Icebergs at the equator

At twilight the view is shaded
What can be seen may seem faded.

Light must be shown
'er we not find our way home.

Science and math are not points of view.
Is there another way of looking at 2 plus 2?

You cannot agree on what you cannot see.
You cannot deny that which meets your eye.

The other side is sometimes just plain wrong.
Sometimes it is not the singer but the damn song.

So stop trying to figure out the other point of view.
Quick! Before more of science they unilaterally undo.

To Inez

The mother of an angel
Must be more
Than an angel herself

A goddess at the least
Or maybe a Meta-angel

Whatever.

Matriarch
Is not the word
The little girl in the picture
Would have used

But that was in 1920

A lot has changed since then.

Lots of people who were SOMEBODY
Are gone and those who are left
Don't rightly remember them.
How many of you know: Booker T,
Marcus Garvey, Walter White, Ralph Bunch, Roy Wilkins?

What has
Not changed
Is love.
Mother love.

Mother love makes you clean other people's homes,
Take care of other people's children,
And go without eating so you can
Clothe, feed, and educate
Your own.

Mother loves teaches you to
Work double shifts,
Drive without stopping

Haul loads men run from

Mother love
Learns you that God
Is stronger than Man
& that men make messes
& that all women don't wear dresses

Mother love
Is hard forgiving
Cause it is hard fighting

Mother love
Knows children need
Fighting for in a world
That don't like black anything
- especially little black girls.

Men come and go
Money comes too few and goes too often
But mother love stays with you

Like the memory of a morning sunrise
Or your first Christmas
Or that first kiss

Mother love stays with you
Like the pain of childbirth

Don't forget that.
Never forget that.

Can't!

Pain
Explains

Why
Mother love
Is hard forgiving

Hard fighting

i.

The hawk woman
hovers
and eyes
those below
who do not know
these little ones
are all she's got.
Without them she is not.
no price too high
no sacrifice too small

they are who she could have been,
would have been,
had she not been
born back
before we were
Black.

When she was no less
than a darky Negress

Nobody remembers
Cause most bodies who do
spent most of their time
trying to forget

Almost a century load of living
outweighs words.

Outliving your friends is no reward.

Somewhere along the way,
one forgets the bad times and
starts to reach the age
where you forget the good times, too.

You begin to live in the
now times
and count your days
by remembering your
grandkids' birthdays
and vowing to give them
their presents in person.

ii

You don't live this long
on hate.
Love is the only thing that fuels
this longevity.
A room full of people who know that
at this very minute
they are where
they are supposed to be…
In the presence of God's angel
sent here ninety years ago
to create the love in this room
to create the strength in this room
to create the promise in this room.

Wealth measured in dollars does not spend in Heaven.
Wealth measured by love does!

An angel is a guardian and protector
of the young and innocent.

The outer orb
of her love circle
is as warm as the inner.

iii.

The mother of the young thief
could never know your pain.
All she knew was her son's longing for

she who would make him complete.

Ella would not stay around
to smooth out her son's rough spots
She would leave the world (and you)
with more children to make right.
And you, along with the world, did that.

On the Mount Rushmore of my mind,
Ella, Sarah, and now you
carve out the monument
to a life well lived
to love well shared.

Family Gathering in Savannah 2015

Wilbert and Gloria Motley (1956)

Christmas 2013

Ella Grisby Motley and Francine,
Sarah Davis Motley and Victoria
Circa 1957

John Motley, Marilyn Motley
Willis, Frank Motley Sr. circa
1952

Thomas, Pops, T.H., and me (1970)

Victoria, Thomas, Francine, Leutrell and me surrounding our mother.

Life On the Curb

I saw a man
Standing on the curb,
Jumping up and down,
From curb to gutter.

I asked him what he was doing.
He answered,
"Practicing."

[For Professor Harry Pratter, Doug Boshkoff & Val Nolan)

The Made Men -

>You have no idea...
>
>How much fun of
>
>Old White Men
>
>I have made.
>
>But I am made of
>
>Old White Men.
>
>And in the quiet
>
>Corner of the Old Library,
>
>I take pride in being
>
>Well made.

Making America Great Again

"Grandpa, what was it like when America was great?"

Holding her hand, looking into those innocent eyes,
The Old Man hesitated:

"America was never great for Black people.
Not when we left Africa on slave ships,
Not when we were sold, the beginning of the apocalypse,
Not when we were "emancipated"
Not when we were "integrated"
Not when we were given the right to vote.
Not when we were given the bogus promissory note.

Not when all your jobs required silence and hard labor.
Not when we were stereotypes that White Folks harbored.

We waited long for our Moses and he came as a King.
Not John the Baptist but the real thing.

The Old Man did not want to tell his grandchildren
About the hard times.
About the go-around-to the-back times.
Your-water-ain't-wet-as-whites-times
He did not want to be reminded of the shine times.
He did not want them to think he was scared.
(He could have fought but ended up dead.)
He did not want them to inherit the hate he had for Whites.
He wanted them to look to the future and assert their rights.
How much of the past they needed to know he was not sure.
He just wanted them to get what they needed and so much more.

And because they did not know what to ask, they asked nothing.
And so nothing they knew.
They hadn't a clue.

So the Old Man gave them books to read.
A token, a morsel to fill their need
Books that spoke of that time.

Books about when being Black was a crime.

As good times follow bad, evil follows the good.
Obama did his best; now see if Trump does, as he should.

But on the *day in 2008*
When Obama was elected,
Perhaps, that was the Day America was Great.

For sure, America was great, the day his grandchildren were born.
For they shall reap the reward from which their forebears were torn.

For Milton
On the Passing of His Father....

Though the father had forgotten
His wonderfulness
As a father,
A husband,
Everyone's friend,
The son remembers.

Occasional walks,
Late night talks,
Understanding silences,
And glances -
Life to tell
In a look.

Father to son.
Father and son.
And now - just the son.

Fathers are rare
Where we come from.
Like somebody ran out of them...

There are no substitutes.
No money back guarantees.
No layaways.

You get one and that's it!

Lucky, we valued
Being valued.
Being loved.
Being done without for.

Evening mourn.
But - in the sun,

As His son,
Go, too,
And be a father.

Baller

On the road to Wall Street,
A Morningside pickup game,
Full of elbows and wolf tickets,
Finger rolls and sweet jumpers,
Turned nasty, then bloody.
By the time the police arrived,
A heart had stopped and
A road map had been torn asunder.
No justice comes from
Death on a basketball court.
Not when the dead are white
And the living are black.
Plea-bargained,
Twenty-year sentence
Won't reverse that.

All we can ever ask
Now or at our last
Is for God to lend an ear
To what we want Him to hear.
- *Anon*

Original G

We share the love
– deep and ever new –
Husky green, heartfelt and true.

The years come and go
Lots we used to know.
Now: not so much so

But this will always be true and dear
Lou Gnerre has a chokehold on God's good ear.

A man among boys,
He understood our noise
And forgave and befriended
Each on our own as God would have intended.

The years have erased
The barriers in place
The wall of class and caste
Was never meant to last.

New Hampton, Fair New Hampton.
(Not always.) But forever
In our hearts as we do our part
To mark the site of our rebirth.
And salute Lou for all we are worth.

Watermelon

I found a faded watercolor
That an old girlfriend gave me.
It was small and was a picture of a cut watermelon.
I do not remember why she gave me the print.
It is nice but not exceptional.
I don't think it was a metaphor for me being a watermelon man.
She was not an AKA – more Delta – so pink and green were not significant colors.
It was not sexual – I don't think –
Me green and she all pink.

That is why I need to write things down.
Memories fade,
Change,
Grow
Slow.

I would ask her
But she probably won't remember either.
Beside, it ended on a bad note:
She got to know me too well.

Still, I keep the print.
It meant something then.
So now, it means something even more.
I just can't remember.

Spanish Driving Lessons

Every time I get behind the wheel,
I practice the lessons she revealed.
Recently in Spain, I fumbled (as I did in class)
For the right word to say, a key phrase for ask.
I have not lived a life without accidents.
But avoided many because her guidance.
My Spanish teacher taught me to drive,
But her life lessons: the point of being alive.

I have lived as she taught me.
Look both ways.
Check the mirror.
Signal your turns,
Big things may be even nearer.
Slowly put on the gas,
And when it is safe:
Move to the left to make your pass.

Life's road - long or short -
The journey is better
For what Jinga taught.

Denise

She always wore black.
As if to be certain
That you made no mistake...

This Blackness
Has its edges.

The doubleness...

Were she white,
Or equal to,
Would she be with us?

Today

We mourn.

She is gone.

We are here,

One warrior short.
And long battles ahead.

Without
The light of her vision,
And the heat from her fire...

Cold relief:
Death.

She touched us all...

Only solace
Is knowing
She considered me
A friend.

The good
She made us do
Is what
Will be missed most.

Homecoming

The Old Library has to give way to the new.
Books are to be read not looked at on IPADS 2.
Classics to be savored - quality lasts.
Kissing in carrels, not fucking under glass.

It is the Principle
(For Carlton)

i

Tardy mornings reveal untidy lives.
We live in the darkness and learn in the light.
In life, one has to adjust – one just must.

ii.

Principal for six,
Married for five,
Parent for two,
The task for the morning was to
Confront this middle schooler
About his fifth late-to-school notice.
The little truant needed to be read the riot act about
Being on time, adhering to the rules,
And not defying school authority.
Not just because he was the principal
But, at 6"2" he was way bigger than the boy and was not about to be trifled with.
On that day, Principal Carlton was in a particularly bad mood because he had an assignment due in his evening master's course: the need for discipline in inner city schools.

Waiting at the door of the school, twenty minutes after the bell, Carlton saw the little miscreant, tiredly walking up to the school. Carlton stood large, looking down on him and in his sternest voice asked: "What's wrong with you? Why are you always late for class?" The little boy looked up at Carlton, who could see in the little boy's eyes that he was trying to decide whether to just take the tongue lashing they both knew was coming or to put down his guard and tell the truth.

"Some days, my mother does not come home. I have to get my three brothers and sisters, dressed, fed, and walked to school."

iii.

Carlton's master course flashed through his mind. He inventoried the chapters he had read.

Nothing.

No best practices to lean upon.

Alone on the limb,
Naked in the arena

On the school yard steps that morning,
The textbook gave way to the good book.

When the head can no longer lead,
One must follow the heart.

You must say the only thing the heart can say to this man-child

"Ok, I understand. You've got to take care of them. After class, you and I need to talk."

iv.

Principal Carlton had lessened the burden but a beast remained.

"Some days, my mother does not come home."

To Sigmund

>Hurrying,
>Sperm of the moment
>Which has changed –
>No, stolen - my life
>And created another anew.
>Moment of madness lost
>Is other's gain.
>Limpid thrust of manhood
>Shriveling up into itself
>As if ashamed.

Who is Cousin Henry?

When told
 "Your grandfather
Was his mother's brother?"

It kinda resonated.
I have a sister and she has a son.

One day I guess that is how
I will be looked upon.

An Evening among Georgia Fir

Going over trees

Contents shifting
Parents slipping
Friends missing
Hearts skipping

It is the Old-timers
For whom there is no regret
Nothing to remember
Nothing to forget

Holding hands once more round the Mulberry bush

"Don't blame us for God letting us live so long"

Contents will shift…

Pollyannaism breaks free
Under Allen wrenching colloquy

Conversations
Resuming in midsentence,
Eloquently accepting,
Not analyzing, friendship's existence

Time on task
Setting standards
That last

Timesharing
Child
Rearing
Parent borrowing
Food preparing

Civil War aha! Is fine.
A plate of food, a glass of wine
Fake no derivatives before its time.

Contents shifting
Going over trees

Émigré of
Acanemic myopia
Refugee of
Navel utopia

By George,
Anyone *can get got*
Few escape having not.

Pacific Palms
Kentucky Psalms
Wisconsin Dells
Savannah Tales

Poems that dare not speak their shame.
Finding an audience to attach my name
Not that you need know it
Nothings wrong with being a poet.

Going over trees
Contents shifting
Parents slipping
Friends missing
Hearts skipping

Puns,
Not peaches,
Teaches.

Dinner at Alecia's

        Alecia cooked
        Rosemary
        Braised
        Lima beans
        With pork chops and
        Lots of Cape Verdean love
        To her guests, long and short past sixty,
        (One of whom deserved to be skewered)
        Imbibed the love in flirtatious conversation,
        Not speaking of the food whose taste dare not be compared.

        A more lovely evening,
        Spent with more beautiful women,
        (Or a less deserving friend)
        Could not be imagined....

        If there is a Food Heaven,
        Alecia's place is assured.
        If the quality of good friends adds points,
        I, too, will get there for sure.

        She may not *want* to be a superwoman
        But her cape is showing.

Jim's Alexis & Me

We are not the machines,
The canes, the walkers,
The pills.

We are the smiles
The mention of our name brings to the face of friends.

Alexis
Love
Connects us.

Your husband, my best friend:
I knew him first but you when friends were thin.

We are not the motley army of pills that besiege the nightstand.

We are the Kodak moment captured in old photographs,
The songs no longer played on the radio,
The memories and secrets only one or two of us know.

I know, but cannot imagine:
Your pain: which is his.
In turn, which is mine.

If tears are prayers,
I did a novena in one morning.
My pillow soaked as I waited for the sun to rise.
Through my friend's eyes, I saw Love's pain.

The insidious reward for living long
Is that things that used to work right,
Start working wrong.

Pain makes us forget
Right from wrong.

We are not what is wrong with us,
But what is right.

We are not the machines, the canes, the pills.

We are more than that.

Tissues

Pocket full of tissues,
You gave me to bear
The avalanche of tears
Of being there.
So near to all he loved.
As close to him
As far from them.
We are all there,
Missing he who was
So strong
For so long.
We never dreamed
(As if a nightmare from hell)
Anything can fell this
Redwood of a man.

But for you,
I could not have made it through
The service.
Fathoming the injustice.
You made me safe
From my grief.
You reminded me
That living in pain
Is worse than Death's release.
Jim in Heaven, his mind at ease.
He lived the good life. Just as he pleased.
He made the best move homeward
For an all ivy NBA power forward.

Lucky

Nine times ten.
Don't know if he could do it again.
Nine times ten.
Living the good life
Married thrice to find the right wife
Nine times ten.
So much has happened to him
Nine times ten.

Splitting the centuries,
World wars and city riots
Human rights and civil wrongs

Revolutions in gender, race, and class
So much has happened, so many questions to ask

His sweetheart turned out not to be.
Southern trees bear strange fruit.
What you try on sometimes is not your suit.
There's a reason she was cold sometimes hot
He being free to be him – and she mysteriously not.
Some unions are not meant to last.
Too much baggage came haunting from the past

When the dust settled,
We were still family.
My uncle, my friend.
Who mentored me
As best he could.
Did right by me
And taught me good.
Guided me from boy to manhood.

Paved the way for me to escape.
Harlem to New Hampshire
Is not an easy journey to make.

I hope it is understood

All that I have done good
Was payment forward
For all the things he stood

Nine times ten.
Living life and trying not to sin
Nine times ten.
So much has happened to him.
Nine times ten.
Glorious things not to be done again
Nine times ten
He has always been lucky
Now and even then.

Grits and Syrup

I did not get why
Big Brother Philip Esco Wilson
Kept asking me about grits and syrup,
Pancakes and jam.

Until the moment he said,
"Strip!"
Lying on the ground,
I felt the first drip –
Syrup.
Then grits.

"Put your clothes back on!"

And then it hit me.
Brother Wilson was not crazy.
He was warning me.
Preparing me.

No skull and bones
Or ivy leaf
Can equal the
Bonds of grits and syrup.

The Alpha - sans Omega of -
Brotherhood.
Forged on Morningside heights
And Hamilton Grange lows.
In the shadow of the
City College gateway,
An all men's convent.

The lions are loose.
John Jay, Furnald, and Carmen too.

Burlap bags, Rhodes scholars, all ivy forwards,

Physics, philosophy, and economics majors.
St. Louis, Brooklyn, New York, Detroit, Chicago -
Black boys from everywhere (you know)

There can be no stronger bond than grits and syrup.
A brotherhood cement, lacquered by ivy leafs and gold trim.

That night, years ago.
When we were too young to appreciate
How much we had left to know...

The submission of our better selves
To the worst of urban strangers
And ivy resenters

On the eve of our first fallen,
We grieve our friend never to be forgotten.
Remembering a night bone chilly,
Grown men doing something so silly.
Every time we get together, we invariably bring it up.
That evening years ago, caked in grits and syrup.

Happy Young

Happy young?
Happy old?

Your story.
You know how
You want it told.

And then it came to pass,
He decided he wanted something that will last.

Your choice.
Whatever makes you moist.

When the mind and body are one.
 Only thing to do is love and have fun.

You choose.
What'cha got to lose?
You make the news!

You chose
Now everybody knows
Platinum is on the shelf
She has Mo' than just herself.

TLC

My kid brother
Now takes care of me.
Repayment for not letting him
Sulk in his guarded youth.

My half
Brother,
Older,
Fuller now,
Once went looking
For his father – not mine –
His brother – not me –

I forgive them both.
Untaught,
They love
Curiously…

All Orphans Are Brothers

The second
Of my borrowed parents died
Five months ago
And their son
Is just telling me.

I don't think he knows
How devastated I am.
He thinks they were just *his* parents.

He never knew how I envied him
The way they smiled when he walked in the room.
How all the dumb things he did, they thought were cute.
And how I would grit my teeth when he would talk about them
Because I knew that parents are the only thing you can't replace.

At best, you borrow
Your friend's
And keep it secret
How much you love them.
Because you miss having parents to love.

And you stay away from your friend
Because you don't trust yourself
Not to try the impossible:
Steal his parents.
Knowing full well
You can't steal parent love.
You can barely borrow it.

But the worst of it,
Absolutely worst,
Is that their death,
Indeed, makes us
Brothers for life.

She

Like her blue jeans,
Never grows old,
Yet,
Is blue –
Blue blooded.
Is soiled –
Sour souled.
Is new –
And newer still
To her family's
Oldness.

Pictures, the clothes

What to do with them?
Some, not worn for years.
Their styles not come round yet.
But, my, how she loved them!

Blue, her favorite color,
Rarely worn to church,
Saved for weddings and new years.

Black-eyed peas,
Champagne and orange juice,
Her favorite tastes.

And what to do with these?
Boxfuls, Faces and Places
- Some I don't know.
Will these strangers keep?
Friends or passer-byes? Closet kin?
Mystery mists a life lived long.

Effects so personal,
Each garment a story.
Every frame a forgotten smell and taste.
Meaning deserted to loss.
What to do – the pictures, the clothes?

Evil Evened

Inching out on the ledge,
Trying to forget
Those who did,
But who forgets
They have children?
How does a child forget?
Having been forgotten?
They accept the pain
& carry on the hurt.
Last tag it to the next generation.
Wound others as they have been wounded.
Punish them for their vulnerability.
"You should have been born stronger/luckier"
My demerits are now yours.
Evil replicated only appears as evil evened.

The Beatitudes

Before I close my eyes
Before I hit the delete key
And create more space in my contacts file,
I keep hearing the grade school refrain,
Subtract the one and carry the two

Life just got a whole lot harder for me
And I didn't know it.

My cousin died last week
And I am trying to carry on
I am trying to imagine
A world where
There is no Bea.

There are those who are always there
In the ether of our lives
Who love you when you aren't looking
Who watch over you when you think you are alone
Who bring you presence at graduation and reunions
Always there. Always remembering. Always cheering..

I took her being for granted.
I did not question her kindness.
I thought I deserved to be
Loved unconditionally.
And she did.

Eighteen hours on the road
And she stood in line
 To say she loved me.

How often did I not call
When only a minute away?

I must forgive myself.
But it is going to be hard.

I mistreated someone
Who loved me.

A world without Bea:
Lonely and cold.

My guardian angel's smile
Her Frankie melody of my name
Reminding me that
To her I was still June's little boy.

Grown up
Means saying goodbye
To those for whom we grew.

Now what do we do?

                ii.

And when Lovye went to Europe
A caramel single and came back
German Chocolate,
Bea stood fast
Against those who said
It wouldn't last.

Four layers later
Trunkful's of new bowling balls and ski attire
The aunt of ever remembered Christmas and birthdays, smiles on nieces and nephews, colorful fruits of God's love.

                iii.

The traveler's sermon from the preacher she hadn't met.

A heart over used
Among a family so huge

Kermit's head and her heart gave out.

When the man you are married to
Is no longer your husband

And when you move back home
To take care of
She who took care of you first
So you will take care of her last.

Or so it was thought. The caregiver
Is not suppose to give out
Before the care giveee

     iv.

There must be trouble in Heaven.
Why else would God send for Bea?

     v.

After the funeral
We all talked, but not about Bea -
(What can be said about the collective hole in our heart?
The abhorred space Nature dare not fill?)

We talked of old friends, fresh fruit, and the good old days.
Our hearts knowing,
The thread of our life unraveled
Needs prayer to mend life's tear

     vi.

She saw three presidents more than me.
I have only one or two left.

Blessed are they that are
Born into the right family:
Blessed are they who are inheritors of Bea's love

For though no one is like Bea,

We must all, nonetheless,
Be like Bea.

We must all and ever:

Float like a butterfly,
            Love like Bea.
                      Float like a butterfly,
                                    Love like Bea.